REDISCOVERING Christmas

REDISCOVERING Christmas

A TWELVE-DAY JOURNEY TO THE MANGER

JOHN GRECO

B&H
PUBLISHING®
BRENTWOOD, TENNESSEE

For Laurin,
the best present I've ever received from the Lord,
and it was on Christmas Eve too!

ACKNOWLEDGMENTS

A book like this comes in fits and starts. It's usually written during time that is carved out of everyday life. Sometimes, that means responsibilities must be set aside for the moment. Other times, it means late nights or early mornings get consumed. Though the actual process of writing is as quiet as the muffled clacking of a laptop keyboard, it can disturb an entire household. So, first and foremost, thanks are due to my wife, Laurin, who indulged me talking about Christmas year round and encouraged me every step of the way. I also want to thank my three boys, Jonah, Jude, and Luke, for giving up their playroom from time to time so Daddy had a place to write—and for all the hugs too!

Thanks to my agent, Teresa Evenson, for encouraging me to write in this direction and for taking this journey with me. Thanks to Caleb for the awesome cover. And thanks to Ashley Gorman and the team at B&H Publishing for their incredible work and support on this project.

Merry Christmas, one and all!

CONTENTS

INTRODUCTION

It's one of the most revered and rehearsed stories of all time, and it's all the more powerful because every word of it is true. The Son of God stepped out of heaven and took up residence in the womb of a teenage girl. He was then born in the small village of Bethlehem, greeted by shepherds, heralded by angels, and later worshipped by wise men from a distant country.

Jesus's birth was the turning point of history, for his earthly life, measured out in a few short decades, culminated with the cross and the empty tomb. But without Christmas, there would be no Easter, and so we mark the occasion every December with songs and celebrations, all to remember the story of our Savior's birth.

But how well do we really know the story as the Bible tells it? With some bits in Matthew and others in Luke, prophecies scattered throughout the Old Testament, and Israel's own history forming the backdrop to Bethlehem, we can easily get lost. The book you are holding in your hands represents a new way to read the Christmas story. Presented as one connected narrative drawn primarily from the Gospels, *Rediscovering Christmas* is a new paraphrase of the biblical account of Jesus's birth.

Since our goal is to get closer to, and go deeper with, the story of the first Christmas as recorded in Scripture, you may be wondering, *Why a paraphrase?* While the intention of most paraphrases is to present the Bible in modern language so today's readers may more easily comprehend it, the goal here is somewhat different. My hope is that as you read the familiar Christmas story anew, it will catch you a bit off guard, not unlike the air when you first step outside on a cold December morning. That's because this paraphrase is more than a mere retelling.

At times, I have gone beyond the conventional confines of a paraphrase. In some instances, I have expanded a word or phrase to provide a fuller sense of the original Greek or Hebrew text; in others, I have done so to draw connections to other portions of God's Word. The early church, steeped in the Hebrew Bible, would have made these connections automatically and even unconsciously, but these links across Scripture are often missed by modern Bible readers. By bringing them to the foreground, my hope is to restore what has been lost.

In addition, there are places where I have added something like "connective tissue" to the narrative. Anyone who's read the Gospels knows that the authors were often sparse in their accounts, leaving readers to draw their own conclusions as to the *why?* or *how?* of a matter. I have sought to incorporate the best of biblical scholarship to fill in some of these gaps.

Interspersed throughout this volume are short articles that offer insights into the cultural background of the biblical Christmas story. In a way, we'll be digging up long-lost artifacts. But the goal is not only to add to our knowledge; it is also to gain a better look at the heart of God. Make no mistake: his heart is there in every verse of Scripture, prodding us toward the Son and calling us back home. And there's no better time than Christmas to come home.

—John Greco

THE WORD BECAME FLESH

(John 1:1–14)

BEFORE THERE WAS TIME, there was the Word of God. And the Word was with God and was God. He was there with God at the beginning of all things. He was the Word spoken at creation, without whom nothing would exist. Within him was life, and that life became the light of true humanity. The light shines on and on. No matter how dark things get, the darkness cannot snuff it out.

There was a man who was given a mission from God. His name was John. His assignment was to tell people about the light so that everyone might believe. Of course, John was not the light; he was merely a man chosen by God to point others to the light. The true and perfect light that shines upon all people was coming into the world.

The God Who Draws Near

Christmas is the answer to the deepest longings of our hearts, longings that have been carried since Eden.

The Word became flesh and dwelt among us. We observed his glory, the glory as the one and only Son from the Father, full of grace and truth. (John 1:14)

In the beginning, God created a good, good world. There was no pain or grief, no hardship or poverty, no loss or heartache. Even better, our first parents, Adam and Eve, enjoyed unbroken fellowship with their heavenly Father. But almost as quickly as the story began, it took a dark turn. In the shade of Eden, Adam and Eve doubted God's good heart, and with the crunch of forbidden fruit, all of creation began to unravel.

However, God did not abandon humanity in their sin. Even as he was doling out consequences and judgments, he made Adam and Eve (and all of us) a promise. He told the serpent, later identified as the devil (Rev. 12:9), "I will put hostility between you and the woman, and between your offspring and her offspring. He will strike your head, and you will strike his heel" (Gen. 3:15). With that word of judgment, God announced a Savior would one day be born, and he would deal evil a fatal blow.

And so, down through the centuries, the people watched and waited, looking for the one God had promised. But they were not left to wait in isolation. God spoke, giving his people instructions and making them promises. At one point, he also came to live with his people, taking up residence in the tabernacle as Israel sojourned in the wilderness and later filling the temple in Jerusalem. But still the people waited for their Savior.

Jesus's arrival was a new chapter in humanity's story, to be sure, but it was also the fulfillment of all the stories the people of Israel had treasured in their hearts. And so, when the apostle John sat down to write his account of the life, death, and resurrection of Jesus of Nazareth, he knew just where to start.

"In the beginning was the Word, and the Word was with God, and the Word was God" (John 1:1). With that opening line, John ushered his readers back to the book of Genesis. There, God brought creation into being by his spoken word. John will introduce his audience to that Word, but first he wants them to consider that the Word is both God and also distinct from God. It won't do to press them together too tightly, nor will it work to pull them apart. It's just like a word that proceeds from your lips— it is both an extension of you and distinct from you. The Word *is* Yahweh, and yet the Word is *with* him. He is sent *from* God, and yet he *is* God.

All that brings us to John's use of "the Word" to describe the Son of God. The prophets of Israel and Judah would sometimes describe revelation they received from God as "the word of the LORD." (See, for example, Gen. 15:1; 1 Sam. 15:10; Ezek. 14:2.) As we read these passages, we commonly think God spoke to these Old Testament saints by a powerful impression or perhaps even with an audible voice, but that's as far as we go. The "word of the LORD" in these instances is a message, nothing more.

But perhaps we're wrong.

Consider Jeremiah 1:4–10. There, Jeremiah records, "The word of the LORD came to me" (v. 4). But then, a few verses later, the prophet tells us, "Then the LORD *reached out his hand, touched my mouth,* and told me: I have now filled your mouth with my words" (v. 9, emphasis added). A disembodied voice, no matter how powerful, does not reach out its hand

and touch someone's mouth. This "LORD" conveying divine words to Jeremiah's mouth was God in physical form.

In John's famous prologue, the Word is a message from the Lord. More accurately, he is the ultimate message, for he is "the radiance of God's glory and the exact expression of his nature" (Heb. 1:3). He came to show us what God is like, to silence any doubts about his goodness. That is why Jesus could say, "The one who has seen me has seen the Father" (John 14:9). But Jesus is more than a message. He descended to be born one of us. He is the offspring God promised to Eve in the garden, the one he said would crush the head of the serpent (Gen. 3:15). He is the God who "camped out" or "tabernacled" with Israel in the wilderness (for that is literally what the Greek word translated "dwelt" in John 1:14 means).

At Christmas, we celebrate the God who draws near, the Savior who came to earth to wipe away our tears, put an end to our grief, and make a way for us to come home. We praise the Word who put on flesh so that he could reach out and touch those he loves. ✦ ✦

READING

One

AN ANSWER
TO PRAYER

(Luke 1:5–25)

A PARAPHRASED RETELLING
OF LUKE 1:5–25

LONG, LONG AGO, when Herod the Great ruled the Jewish homeland, there lived a priest of God named Zechariah. Now, Zechariah was a Levite, and he could trace his family line all the way back to the beginning of the priesthood, through the family of Abijah, to the first high priest, Aaron, the brother of Moses. Zechariah's wife, Elizabeth, had quite a heritage as well. She, too, could follow the branches of her family tree back to Aaron. But a common ancestor wasn't all Zechariah and Elizabeth shared. Together, they loved the Lord and followed his Word closely, being faithful to obey his commands and walk in his ways. If there was anything missing from their lives, it was this: they had no children. When Elizabeth was younger, she had been unable to conceive, and now it was too late—she and Zechariah were too old to have a baby.

One day, while Zechariah's priestly division was serving at the temple complex in Jerusalem, Zechariah was chosen by lot to enter the holy place and burn incense to the Lord. It was a once-in-a-lifetime honor, and people gathered outside to pray as Zechariah attended to his sacred task.

While Zechariah was in that hallowed room, there appeared the most wondrous sight. Just to the right of the altar stood an angel of the Lord! Zechariah quivered. His knees went weak. He might have passed out from dread if the angel hadn't spoken up: "Don't be frightened, Zechariah! Your prayer has reached the throne room of heaven. God has heard it! Your wife, Elizabeth, is going to have a baby, the son you've always wanted! Call him John. He will bring tremendous joy and happiness to you, and not only to you—many people will celebrate his arrival. God himself will consider him a great man. In fact, he'll be set apart for service to the Lord all his days. He must not have any wine or strong drinks because, before he's even born, he will be filled with something—or rather someone—far more potent, the Holy Spirit of God!

"This John of yours will bring many of Israel's sons and daughters back to God. He will go on ahead of the Lord, preparing the way. He will have the same spirit and power as the prophet Elijah. Just as Malachi promised, he will be the 'Elijah' who turns the hearts of fathers toward their children and shows the disobedient how to get back on the path of wisdom and faithfulness. And he'll do all this to get people prepared for the coming of the Lord."

Zechariah was in shock, and in that moment, he gave voice to the doubts swirling around in his heart. He said to the angel, "How can I know what you're telling me will really happen? I'm too old, and so is Elizabeth."

The angel responded with the resolve of heaven: "I am Gabriel—the same Gabriel you've read about in the book of Daniel—and I stand before Almighty God. He sent me to you, to bring you the good news I have just delivered. But now, since you did not believe *my* words, you will be without *yours*. You will be unable to speak until your doubts are finally put to rest, until these things I have spoken come to pass and you are able to hold the child that has been promised to you, this gift of God."

Back outside, the people waited, curious as to why it was taking Zechariah so long to burn the incense and offer up a prayer for the nation. When Zechariah finally joined them, he walked slowly and in complete silence. It didn't take the people long to discover it wasn't just that Zechariah *wasn't* speaking; it was that he *couldn't* speak. Zechariah did his best to mime what had happened. The crowd put two and two together and concluded that the old priest had seen a vision while he was inside the temple.

Soon the week of temple service was over, and Zechariah returned home to the hill country, to his wife, Elizabeth, unable to speak or hear. In due time, Elizabeth did indeed become pregnant, just as Gabriel had promised. For five whole months, though, she kept the amazing and miraculous news to herself. After all, who would believe her until her pregnancy was undeniable? "The Lord has smiled upon me," she told herself. "Now that I am carrying this child within me, he has taken away the shame and disappointment I used to carry!" ✦

Two Prayers with a Single Answer

God wasn't just answering Zechariah's prayer for a child; he was also answering a nation's longing for peace.

But the angel said to him, "Do not be afraid, Zechariah, because your prayer has been heard. Your wife Elizabeth will bear you a son, and you will name him John." (Luke 1:13)

It's not difficult to imagine that as the years went by and they were still without a child to hold in their arms, Zechariah and Elizabeth stopped praying for one. At a certain age, they must have taken God's silence as the answer they had dreaded hearing. And so, when Zechariah was chosen to burn incense in the temple, it's unlikely he took the opportunity to pray, once more, for a baby.

The prayer Zechariah offered that day wasn't about his family or his personal needs; instead it was a prayer made in true priestly fashion—on behalf of all Israel. As a priest, he likely prayed for God to remember the promises he made to his people long ago, promises to rescue them from their oppressors and to send the Messiah to bring peace and justice to all the earth.

Similar prayers had been made thousands of times down through the centuries by other priests standing in the same sacred spot in the temple, but Zechariah was the only one to receive an immediate response delivered by an envoy from heaven. And yet, God's answer seemed to have more to do with the longings of Zechariah and Elizabeth than the long-ings of the nation.

But that's only the way it seemed.

God's answer was big enough to satisfy both prayers. Zechariah and Elizabeth's long heartache would soon turn to joy as they welcomed a son in their old age. But that son wouldn't merely be another Jewish boy in the line of Aaron; he would be the forerunner of the Messiah, the one to prepare God's people for the coming of the Lord.

In ancient Israel, a priest's job was to be a mediator between God and man. That job John would do, though he wouldn't serve in the temple or offer animal sacrifices. Rather, he would be "a voice of one crying out in the wilderness" (Mark 1:3), charging his fellow Israelites to offer the sacrifice God truly desires, "a broken and humbled heart" (Ps. 51:17). And he wouldn't stand in the way between God and his people to act as an intercessor. Instead, he would prepare the way for God's Son to live among his people.

With Gabriel's announcement to Zechariah, a new age dawned. John would set the stage for Jesus's ministry, and Jesus would, in turn, bring light to the darkness, hope to the hurting, and salvation to sinners. All those years, Zechariah and Elizabeth thought they were praying a simple prayer for a child, but in God's purposes, the answer they longed for became a miracle that changed absolutely everything. ♦ ♦

READING

Two

THE SON OF
GOD PROMISED

(Luke 1:26–38)

A PARAPHRASED RETELLING
OF LUKE 1:26-38

IN THE SIXTH MONTH of Elizabeth's pregnancy, God gave the angel Gabriel a new assignment. He sent his messenger to a young woman named Mary in the small village of Nazareth in Galilee. Now, Mary was a virgin, and she was pledged to be married to Joseph, a noble man born of a noble line, the house and family of King David. The angel appeared to Mary and said to her: "Rejoice! God has poured out his grace upon you, and he is with you!"

Mary was unsettled by this greeting, and she tried to make sense of it. Gabriel, seeing her struggle, continued, "Don't be alarmed, Mary, for God delights in you! You will soon be pregnant and have a Son, and you are to name him Jesus—'Yahweh is salvation!' He will be a man above all others, and he will be known as the Son of God Most High. What's more, Yahweh will give him the throne of his ancestor King David, and he will reign over Israel forever. That's right—his kingdom will have no end."

Overwhelmed, Mary just had to say something: "But wait—how can this be? I've never been with a man. I can't become pregnant."

Gabriel nodded his head knowingly. "God's Spirit will come upon you, and God's power will be your covering. That is why this child will be known not only as your Son but also as the holy Son of God. Think about your cousin Elizabeth for a moment. As you well know, by every measure she is too old to have a child, and yet she is now six months pregnant. I tell you—nothing is impossible with God!"

Mary took in all that the angel had told her. Then she bowed her head and spoke: "Here I am, a willing servant of the Lord. May everything you have just said come to pass."

His message now delivered, Gabriel left almost as suddenly as he had arrived. ✦

The Original "Virgin" Birth

Isaiah's prophecy of a virgin birth had more than one fulfillment, but the wording reveals God's sovereign hand.

"Therefore, the Lord himself will give you a sign: See, the virgin will conceive, have a son, and name him Immanuel." (Isa. 7:14)

God is a gracious God, and he proves it over and over again. Take, for example, the case of King Ahaz of Judah. Ahaz had thumbed his nose at Yahweh every chance he got. Even though he sat on the throne in Jerusalem, he rejected the Lord's ways and worshipped the dark gods of the region with gusto. He even went so far as to give his son to those demons as a burnt offering (see 2 Kings 16:3). And yet, in spite of Ahaz's wickedness, God promised to protect the king and his kingdom.

When armies from Israel and Aram invaded Judah and threatened to topple Jerusalem, the Lord sent his servant, the prophet Isaiah, to speak to the king. Isaiah made clear that these nations that had risen up against Judah would fail in their endeavor. Ahaz didn't have to do anything, only trust this word from God. And to help him cultivate that trust, the Lord made Ahaz a generous offer: "Ask for a sign from the LORD your God—it can be as deep as Sheol or as high as heaven" (Isa. 7:11). In other words, God was willing to give the foolish king a sign of his choosing—any sign at all—so he would know God was faithful to keep his word.

Ahaz could have asked for the sky to turn pink at midnight, and God would have done it. He could have asked for fish to fly and birds to swim,

He was in the world—the world he was instrumental in creating—and yet no one recognized who he was. He came to a people he had claimed as his own centuries earlier, and yet they refused to claim him. But to those who did claim him, to those who recognized who he was and put their faith in him, he granted the power to become God's children. These were not children born of natural means, but children born of God.

The Word of God became flesh and bone and made himself at home in the midst of our camp. We saw his glory and felt its weight—the glory of the one and only Son, sent by the Father, brimming with grace and truth. ✦

and God would have granted his desire. Whatever Ahaz wanted, God would have complied; he only wanted the king to trust him. It was an invitation like no other. But Ahaz, true to form, refused to ask for a sign. He wasn't interested in knowing the Lord, let alone trusting him.

That's when Isaiah uttered the words we hear every Christmas: "Therefore, the Lord himself will give you a sign: See, the virgin will conceive, have a son, and name him Immanuel" (7:14). Most of us automatically jump to Mary and Jesus and the manger and the shepherds when we read this prophecy. But there was another "virgin" birth, another fulfillment of this promise given long before the Son of God put on flesh and made his home among us. We know this because Isaiah promised stubborn Ahaz that this prophesied child would still be a young boy when the nations challenging Judah were reduced to nothing (vv. 15–16). It would be another seven hundred years before Jesus would be placed in that manger in Bethlehem, so clearly there was a first child in view to fulfill this prophecy in part before the final child—the Christ child—came to fulfill it completely.

This other boy was Isaiah's own son (see 8:3), though of course Isaiah's wife—simply called "the prophetess"—was not a virgin. But she didn't have to be. The Hebrew word *almah*, translated "virgin" in most English versions of Isaiah 7:14, is better understood as "young woman." The term was often used of women who were still young but old enough to get married. So, though the term does not demand it, most of the women who could be referred to as an *almah* were still virgins. (This is why, centuries later, when the Hebrew Bible was translated into Greek, scribes chose the word *parthenos*, the technical term for a virgin, as a stand-in for *almah*.)

While Isaiah's wife was certainly not a virgin, it's a peculiar thing that *almah* was chosen. Why did Isaiah's choice of wording, as inspired by the Holy Spirit, include a word that implies a virgin would give birth? Why not simply say that a *woman* would conceive? The answer is that God always had a double fulfillment in view, and so the Spirit inspired a word that was flexible enough to bear the weight of both promised births.

In the end, the coward Ahaz sought help from Tiglath-Pileser, the king of Assyria, rather than God. The Assyrian army did indeed come to his rescue, obliterating Syria and Israel in due time. But Ahaz was forced to pay tribute (read: protection money) to Tiglath-Pileser year after year. In essence, he forced his own people to become slaves to a foreign nation. He did this because he could not bring himself to trust God.

Ahaz thought it best to solve his own problems, to take care of things himself, rather than yield himself to the Lord of heaven and earth. As pitiful a man as Ahaz was, he was not unique. Countless others have followed the same broken path. And yet, the sign God gave to Ahaz came with a message: *Immanuel*, or "God with us." God promised to be with his people. He would not abandon them to their enemies.

Of course, the title *Immanuel*, when applied to Jesus, took on a much deeper meaning. God the Son became a man and lived among us. And while that is utterly amazing, equally amazing is that the Holy Spirit—the Spirit of Jesus—now lives inside each one of his followers. Jesus himself said, "If anyone loves me, he will keep my word. My Father will love him, and we will come to him and make our home with him" (John 14:23). And so, today God is with us *and* within us, comforting us, empowering us, and reassuring our hearts that no evil scheme, no matter how diabolical, can separate us from his love. ✦ ✦

READING

Three

SHARED JOY
IN THE HILL COUNTRY

(Luke 1:39–56)

A PARAPHRASED RETELLING
OF LUKE 1:39–56

BEFORE LONG, YOUNG MARY decided she needed to see her cousin Elizabeth, perhaps the only person in the world who might understand some small measure of what she was feeling. Not wasting any time, she got up, left home, and joined a caravan traveling to Judea.

When Mary's journey was over, she entered the house and greeted Elizabeth. And when Mary's warm words reached her cousin's ears, the baby in Elizabeth's womb leaped for joy. Instantly, Elizabeth was filled with the Holy Spirit and began to prophesy loudly, "Of all women, you are blessed! Blessed, too, is the baby growing in your womb! What could I have possibly done to deserve such an honor—to have the mother of my Lord come to see me? The moment I heard your voice, the baby in my womb began to jump and kick from pure joy. God's blessings are all yours, Mary, for you believed everything he revealed to you!"

It was all too much for Mary, and she could no longer hold back her praise:

> My soul lives to make much of God, and my spirit radiates joy because of God my Savior!

> He looked down from heaven on this humble girl—and now, for all time, I will be known as God's favored one!

> The God who can do all things has done incredible things for me!

> The name of Yahweh is like no other; it is holy beyond measure.

> His mercy extends to all who fear him, year after year, generation after generation without end.

> With the fierceness of a warrior, he has sent the proud running in every direction,

all those who imagine they are more than they really are.

He has toppled the thrones of the rich and powerful, and has lifted up the humble.

He has satisfied the hungry with the best food—all they could eat—but he has sent the wealthy and self-reliant away with nothing.

He has come to Israel's rescue, remembering his mercy and the forever promises he made to Abraham and his children.

And so, Mary stayed with Zechariah and Elizabeth for the next three months, and after that time, she returned home to Nazareth. ✦

. . . .

How Christmas Was Saved from the Start

. . . .

This is the true tale of how one mom single-handedly saved Christmas from being lost to history.

And Mary said: "My soul magnifies the Lord. . . . He has helped his servant Israel, remembering his mercy to Abraham and his descendants forever, just as he spoke to our ancestors." (Luke 1:46, 54–55)

We are a people of *now*. Our time on this earth is short, so we are fixated on what happens today and next week, or perhaps if we stretch ourselves to be forward-thinking, we might consider what life will look like in the summer. Rarely do we think about the generation that will be alive thirty years from now, much less a hundred. We are concerned primarily with the present.

Not so with God. Yes, he cares about the details of our lives, and he desires that we walk in step with his Spirit throughout this present day. But he also looks across time to next year and next century and next millennium. That is why he can say, "I declare the end from the beginning, and from long ago what is not yet done" (Isa. 46:10). God dwells in eternal light, outside of time, while also being the one in whom "we live and move and have our being" (Acts 17:28), here with us (and within us) as time ticks forward moment by moment. Needless to say, God is not impatient like we are.

This difference in perspective is why our prayers normally aim at the immediate and the soon-to-be and why it often seems to us God is slow in answering our petitions. It must have seemed that way for the count-less Old Testament saints who longed to greet God's promised Messiah.

The prophet Zechariah looked down through the centuries and saw the King ride into Jerusalem on a donkey (Zech. 9:9), and more than five hundred years came and went before Jesus arrived on history's stage. Likewise, Isaiah spoke of a Son who would be born of a virgin (Isa. 7:14), one upon whose shoulders the government of the world would rest (9:6), and it was seven hundred years before Jesus was placed in a manger in Bethlehem. Then there's David, who wanted to know the Lord who would sit at God's right hand and judge the nations (Ps. 110:1, 5–6), this descen-dant who would ensure his own kingdom would last forever (2 Sam. 7:16). But it would be a thousand years before Jesus would find a spot on David's family tree. There was Abraham, who looked up into the night sky and tried to count the stars, knowing God had promised him descen-dants just as numerous (Gen. 15:5). Two thousand years later, Jesus would be one of those descendants, the one through whom all nations on earth would be blessed. Even Adam and Eve waited on a promise from the Lord: the offspring who would crush the head of the serpent and destroy evil, once and for all (Gen. 3:15).

To say there was anticipation concerning the coming of the Messiah would be an understatement. In the years leading up to the events of the first Christmas, there was nothing short of a fervor throughout Israel. And yet, when Jesus did show up—when all those long-standing, heavenly promises about the coming Savior-King *finally* dropped down in the person of Christ— he did so without public fanfare. His birth was revealed to a short list: Mary and Joseph, Zechariah and Elizabeth, a few shepherds local to Bethlehem, wise men from the East, and old-timers Simeon and Anna. Yes, the sky lit up with an angelic host announcing the birth of the Savior, but the audience for this event consisted of sheep and their caretakers. Even the star in the sky that proclaimed a new King had entered the world was only understood by magi from a faraway land. (More on these stories later!)

When you step back and think about it, the cast of Christmas is really a strange bunch, and most of them were gone before either Matthew or Luke sat down to write their accounts of Jesus's birth. Zechariah and Elizabeth were already old when John was born, and surely they died before Jesus and John grew up. Likewise, Simeon and Anna were advanced in years, and they must have gone home to be with the Lord shortly after seeing baby Jesus in the temple. The shepherds returned to their fields after that special night in Bethlehem. And the wise men, after seeing the two-year-old Jesus for themselves, ventured home. As far as we can tell, they never returned to the promised land. Sadly, Joseph appears to have died sometime before Jesus began his earthly ministry. He's not mentioned in the Gospels after Jesus's excursion to the temple at age twelve. Joseph's passing is the most likely reason the citizens of Nazareth referred to Jesus as "the son of Mary" (Mark 6:3).

Speaking of Mary, it's safe to say that if it weren't for Jesus's mom, Christmas would now be lost to the ages. She was the one who experienced that first Christmas and "was treasuring up all these things in her heart and meditating on them" (Luke 2:19), and she was the only one left standing when it was time for the Gospels to be written. Therefore, she must have been the one who told Luke about the shepherds and relayed their story about the angelic announcement. She must also have been the one who told Matthew about Joseph's dreams and the star that brought dignitaries from the East. All of God's people should have recognized Jesus as the way God kept his many promises about a coming Savior-King, but in the end, it was Mary who recognized, believed, and declared that God was rescuing the world in Christ, "just as he spoke to our ancestors" (Luke 1:55).

Mary saved Christmas for all of us. So, while only a few people celebrated Jesus when he first came into this world, thanks to Mary, billions of people around the world today rehearse the old, old story and thank God for sending his Son to be King and Savior—to be present with us today and for all eternity. ✦ ✦

READING

Four

HIS NAME
IS JOHN

(Luke 1:57–79)

A PARAPHRASED RETELLING
OF LUKE 1:57–79

WHEN THE TIME CAME, Elizabeth gave birth to a son, just as the angel Gabriel had promised. Family and friends rejoiced with her, and everyone celebrated God's great mercy. When the baby was eight days old, it was time to circumcise him, according to the instructions God had given to Moses. All the close friends and relatives who had gathered for the occasion wanted to name the boy Zechariah, after his father, but Elizabeth wouldn't have it. "No," she said resolutely, "he's going to be named John."

"But no one in the family has that name," they told her.

Then, all eyes turned to Zechariah, and several people made gestures to ask him what he wanted the child to be named. The old man motioned for a writing tablet and, to everyone's surprise, scrawled, "His name is John."

At that moment, Zechariah's speech was restored—his mouth opened, his tongue loosened, and he began praising God. Awe and wonder fell upon the whole village, and news of what the Lord had done spread throughout the hill country of Judea. Everyone who heard about these things wondered about the baby. "What will he become?" they asked one another. It was obvious to all that the hand of God was upon the boy.

Zechariah was filled with the Holy Spirit and, with his voice now returned to him, made a prophetic declaration:

> Praise Yahweh, the God of Israel! He has come to redeem his people!
>
> He has raised up a powerful Savior from the house of his servant David.
>
> All this was spoken by the prophets long ago.

They foretold our salvation from our enemies and our deliverance from the clutches of all who despise us.

Through these prophets, God promised our ancestors the mercy we are now receiving; he has remembered his holy covenant!

He has not forgotten the promise he made to our father Abraham—to rescue us from our enemies and set us free to worship him boldly and without fear.

With holy and pure lives, we can live in God's presence both now and forever!

And you, little one, you will be known as a prophet of almighty God, for you have been commissioned to prepare the path for his arrival.

You have been tasked with declaring the way of salvation to his people so that their sins might be forgiven in a torrent of God's tender mercy!

The sun is rising in the heavens; its light is coming to us.

Its brightness will reveal those who dwell in darkness, who live under death's shadow, but it will also guide our steps onto the path of peace. ✦

What's in a Name?

God is gracious, and his good gifts never disappoint.

*He has dealt mercifully with our ancestors and remembered his holy
covenant—the oath that he swore to our father Abraham, to grant that
we, having been rescued from the hand of our enemies, would serve him
without fear in holiness and righteousness in his presence all our days.*
(Luke 1:72–75)

It must have been difficult for Zechariah and Elizabeth. Day after day,
year after year, hoping and praying for a child to call their own. They
would celebrate with family and friends whenever a new baby was born,
but it was never their turn. They would remember the Scriptures—how
God brought a miracle son to Sarah in her old age, how God opened the
wombs of women like Rachel and Hannah—and they would pray, hoping
he would do the same for them.

Even when talking to each other, Zechariah and Elizabeth were reminded
of what they had not yet received from the hand of God. Elizabeth's name
means "my God is an oath." And while it's true that God had not made
an oath to give Zechariah and Elizabeth a child, he had promised to
make Abraham into a great nation:

> *He took him outside and said, "Look at the sky and count the stars,
> if you are able to count them." Then he said to him, "Your offspring
> will be that numerous." (Gen. 15:5)*

After decades had passed, Zechariah and Elizabeth must have looked up at the stars in the night sky above Judea and thought, *I guess none of those are for us.* God had fulfilled his oath to Abraham, but he had apparently decreed that their branch of the family tree would grow no further.

Then there's Zechariah. His name means "Yahweh remembers." But from where he stood, it must have seemed that Yahweh had forgotten about him. All those prayers, and there was never an answer—or perhaps the answer was simply no. Either way, Zechariah must have wondered why. Maybe he wrestled with God, pleading for a blessing, like Jacob before him (Gen. 32:24–32). But the limp Zechariah walked away with could not be seen. It was an ache in his heart that he carried with him for years and years.

And so, it may be that when Elizabeth called out, "Zechariah! Come for supper!" he was reminded "Yahweh remembers!" and wondered if he really did. Every time Zechariah told his wife, "Elizabeth, I love you," she may have thought to herself, *My God is an oath, just not for me.*

But their story didn't end there. In the temple in Jerusalem, the angel Gabriel brought Zechariah the wonderful news that Elizabeth would soon become pregnant. And true to his word, God gave Zechariah and Elizabeth the child they had always dreamed about. Perhaps to correct any false perceptions about God that may have sprung up in their hearts during the long years of disappointment, Gabriel told Zechariah to name the child John, which means "Yahweh is gracious."

Indeed he is.

Not only had God answered the prayers of Zechariah and Elizabeth with the gift of a son, that son would prepare the way for the Messiah, Jesus of Nazareth, who is the fulfillment of all of God's promises. "For every one of God's promises is 'Yes' in him" (2 Cor. 1:20).

After spending at least nine months unable to speak, Zechariah received his voice back, and the first thing he did was praise the Lord. It is likely not a coincidence that in the midst of his prophetic declaration, he spoke these words:

> *He has dealt mercifully with our ancestors and* **remembered** *his holy covenant—***the oath** *that he swore to our father Abraham, to grant that we, having been rescued from the hand of our enemies, would serve him without fear in holiness and righteousness in his presence all our days.* (Luke 1:72–75, emphasis added)

Yahweh remembered. He kept his oath. Holding their little boy in their arms—the one God chose to prepare the way for the Messiah—Zechariah and Elizabeth understood that Yahweh is indeed gracious, more gracious than they could have ever imagined. ✦ ✦

READING

Five

AN EARTHLY FATHER FOR
A HEAVENLY SON

(Matthew 1:18–25)

A PARAPHRASED RETELLING
OF MATTHEW 1:18–25

BACK IN NAZARETH, MARY'S pregnancy was progressing. This left Joseph, the man she was pledged to marry, with a gut-wrenching decision to make. Mary had told her beloved the truth—that her pregnancy was the work of the Holy Spirit—but Joseph couldn't swallow it. It was too amazing, too unusual, for him to believe. And so, because he was a good man, he decided to divorce Mary privately; the last thing he wanted to do was put the woman he loved through a public ordeal that would expose her to scorn and shame.

Joseph's heart was heavy with this decision, but his mind was made up. That night, however, he had the most astonishing dream—a dream he knew at once was more than just a dream. An angel appeared to him and said, "Joseph, of David's noble line, you have nothing to fear in taking Mary to be your wife. The child in her womb is indeed from the Holy Spirit. When the time comes, she will give birth to a baby boy. I want you to give him the name *Jesus*. It's a fitting name—'Yahweh is salvation!'—because he will save his people from the ravages of their sins."

Joseph quickly realized that in deciding what to do about Mary and her pregnancy, he had been so focused on the Law that he had forgotten about the Prophets. But this was just what the prophet Isaiah had announced centuries earlier: "The virgin will become pregnant and give birth to a Son. He will be called Immanuel—God with us!" When Joseph woke up, he acted in faith, believing everything the angel had said. Without delay, he took Mary home with him to be his wife, though of course they remained pure until Mary gave birth to her Son. ✦

God's Provision for Mary

While some may assume Mary was ridiculed and shamed for becoming pregnant prior to her marriage, the Bible suggests this may not be the case.

So her husband, Joseph, being a righteous man, and not wanting to disgrace her publicly, decided to divorce her secretly. (Matt. 1:19)

All the way back in Eden, Adam and Eve made a choice that ushered sin and death into our world. Suddenly, the peace and wholeness they knew was shattered. They looked at their bodies and, with their innocence lost, felt shame because of their nakedness. They tried to conceal themselves with fig leaves, but that wasn't much of a solution. So God, in his grace, provided animal skins for the couple and covered their shame. Even though they had disobeyed his command and eaten the forbidden fruit, twisting his good creation in the process, Yahweh still provided for their needs. That's how good he is.

Fast-forward millennia and head to the small village of Nazareth. There, a teenage girl is not yet fully married and is pregnant with a child who does not belong to her beloved. Imagine the shame she feels as people stare at her. Consider the scorn she endures, day in and day out, as her growing belly becomes a scandal in town.

Countless sermons have been preached exhorting us to follow Mary's example and endure shame for the sake of obedience. Sometimes that's simply the cost of following the Lord, they say. It's part of living the

Christian life in a broken world, they assure us. That's not a bad message, of course; Jesus said we should expect difficulty and ridicule sometimes (Matt. 10:22; John 16:33) and that those who suffer for righteousness will be blessed (Matt. 5:10–12). There's only one problem with taking that angle with Mary's story though: it simply isn't true.

Despite popular retellings of the Christmas story, there's no indication that Mary suffered a minute of shame because of her Holy-Spirit-induced pregnancy. Luke tells us that shortly after Mary conceived, she left town for three months to stay with her cousin Elizabeth in Judea (Luke 1:39–56). If she experienced morning sickness during her first trimester, it was there in Elizabeth and Zechariah's home—not in Nazareth, where people might suspect something. Then, sometime after returning to Nazareth, she told Joseph about her unique situation. While Matthew's Gospel doesn't tell us how far along Mary was at that point, it's safe to assume it wasn't too long after she got back into town. We're told, "It was *discovered* . . . that she was pregnant" (Matt. 1:18, emphasis added). In other words, her pregnancy was beginning to show, and she couldn't hide it from Joseph any longer. If Mary was like most women, this would have been shortly after her third month of pregnancy.

Even with her body changing, it's clear that the townspeople did not realize she was pregnant. We know this because Joseph planned to divorce her discreetly, "not wanting to disgrace her publicly" (v. 19). There would have been no point in pursuing a quiet divorce if the whole village already knew she was pregnant. But of course, Joseph did not go through with the divorce at all. An angel appeared to him in a dream and told him the child was conceived by the Holy Spirit. "When Joseph woke up, he did as the Lord's angel had commanded him. He married her" (v. 24). From that point on, if word of Mary's pregnancy had gotten out, there would have been little chance of a scandal, for she was a newly married young woman. And with the loose-fitting clothing of the era, her body shape would have remained her own business.

When her pregnancy progressed, she left town once again. This time, she headed to Judea with Joseph. Contrary to the many modern depictions of Mary going into labor the night they reached Bethlehem, Luke doesn't tell us how long the couple was in town before Mary's contractions began. It may have been days, weeks, or even months. And because none of their neighbors from Nazareth were there, no one could do the calendar math and figure out she had gotten pregnant three months prior to her marriage to Joseph.

But even if we weren't able to plot Mary's pregnancy time line using these details from Scripture, there's another good reason to believe Mary was never an object of scorn and derision. During Jesus's ministry, he attracted crowds wherever he went, but he also attracted lots of opposition. His enemies—local religious leaders and the priestly elite in Jerusalem—were always looking for a way to bring him down:

- They pointed out that Jesus was from Galilee and that no Old Testament passage promised a prophet from that region (John 7:52; although see Isa. 9:1–2).
- They called him "a glutton and a drunkard, a friend of tax collectors and sinners!" (Matt. 11:19).
- Time and time again, they accused him of breaking the Sabbath because he healed people on Saturday (Luke 6:6–11; John 5:18; 9:16).
- Perhaps worst of all, they accused him of driving out demons by harnessing the power of Satan (Matt. 12:24).

These wicked men hurled every lie and false allegation they could throw at Jesus, but they never castigated him for being conceived out of wedlock. Had Mary's pregnancy been scandalous, rumors would have spread, and when Jesus rose to prominence, his enemies would surely have used the buzzworthy stories to attack him.

Taken together, these details help us conclude that instead of allowing Mary to bear shame in carrying the Messiah, God likely spared Mary from shame. As he had done in Eden, the Lord provided a covering for a beloved daughter. And years later, she and Joseph were able to return home to Nazareth with Jesus, who was a toddler by that point (Matt. 2:21–23). Any questions about the timing of her pregnancy would have been swept away by the intervening years, and Mary would be able to look back on those nine months with joy, remembering how God took care of every detail. ✦ ✦

READING

Six

THE BIRTH
OF HOPE

(Luke 2:1–7)

A PARAPHRASED RETELLING
OF LUKE 2:1–7

AS JOSEPH AND MARY were preparing to welcome the promised child into the world, their waiting was suddenly interrupted. Caesar Augustus issued a decree that affected nearly everyone in the Roman Empire, including them. (This was the first census, the one that took place while Quirinius was still governor of Syria.) The head of every household was required to return to his ancestral home to register. For Joseph, that meant traveling from Nazareth in Galilee south to Bethlehem in Judea, the hometown of David, his ancestor.

Joseph and Mary made the trip together, uncomfortable though it was for Mary in her pregnant state. While they were there in Bethlehem, Mary went into labor, and she gave birth to her firstborn child, a Son.

Since the guest room in the home where they were staying was full, Mary made do with what was available in the lower part of the house; she swaddled the baby and placed him in a feeding trough to sleep. ✦

The Inn That Wasn't

When we correct one small misunderstanding about "the inn" where Jesus was born, the night of his birth becomes radically different.

Then she gave birth to her firstborn son, and she wrapped him tightly in cloth and laid him in a manger, because there was no guest room available for them. (Luke 2:7)

It's a scene that nativity plays and holiday specials have made all too familiar: Joseph and Mary arrive in Bethlehem late at night. Mary's contractions have begun, and Joseph searches desperately for a place where they can stay. When they finally arrive at the only inn in town, the innkeeper tells the couple he's booked solid; there isn't a single room left. Seeing their plight, however, he can't turn them away. He thinks for a moment and remembers the old stable out back. Technically, even that room isn't vacant—there are animals inside keeping warm—but it's better than sleeping in the street, he assures his guests. And so, left with little choice, Mary and Joseph make the best of a bad situation and settle in for the night. A few hours of unmedicated labor later, Mary delivers a baby boy. With no crib or cradle to be found, she lays him down to sleep in a manger.

It's a powerful scene, but there's one small problem with it: most of it almost certainly didn't happen. Luke's account is sparse, and much of our shared understanding of that special night comes to us from inference based on certain translations of a particular verse. In some translations, Luke 2:7 tells us that after Mary birthed Jesus, she wrapped him in swaddling clothes and laid him in a manger *"because there was no room for them in the inn"* (KJV, emphasis added).[1]

The Greek word translated as "inn" in this verse is *katalyma*, but it's better translated as "guest room."[2] We know this because elsewhere in his Gospel, in the parable of the good Samaritan, Luke uses a different Greek word to describe an "inn" (10:34). And he uses *katalyma* with reference to the upper room where Jesus and his disciples gathered for their Last Supper together (22:11). Add to that the fact that history tells us ancient Bethlehem was too far from any major roads to support public lodging,[3] and the inn disappears completely from the story.

Without the scene of rejection at a local inn, there is no reason to believe Mary went into labor on the very night she and Joseph arrived in town. Luke simply says it happened "while they were there" (Luke 2:6). Most likely, Mary and Joseph were staying with family. After all, they were both from the line of David, and so they both had family ties to Bethlehem. And because so many people were in town for the census, the upper guest room—the *katalyma*—in the house where they were staying was occupied.

Mary was given a more comfortable room in which to labor, the same room on the main floor of the home that housed animals on cold nights. That's why there was a manger laying around. Of course, the presence of a feeding trough doesn't mean Mary and Joseph were surrounded by sheep, goats, and chickens. It just means that, at some point (not necessarily that night), there had been farm animals in the house.

The loss of the inn is a small tweak to the Christmas story we've heard so many times, but it's one that alters almost everything we think we know about the night Jesus was born. Mary didn't have to fight against a hostile world to deliver the Son of God. Instead, God took tender care of her—the woman he had chosen above all others to be the mother of his Son. This first picture of Christmas is a humble one, but it isn't one of hardship and destitution. It's instead filled with the Lord's marvelous provision. ✦ ✦

READING

Seven

ANGELS AND SHEPHERDS AND AN ANCIENT PROPHECY FULFILLED

(Luke 2:8–20; Isaiah 9:6–7)

A PARAPHRASED RETELLING
OF LUKE 2:8–20 AND ISAIAH 9:6–7

OUT IN THE NEARBY FIELDS, shepherds were up late into the night, keeping watch over their flocks. All of a sudden, the darkness was pierced by the glory of God, and these lowly shepherds found themselves face-to-face with an angel of the Lord.

Naturally, the shepherds were terrified. But the angel sought to calm their fears: "Don't be scared! I come with good news, news that will bring joy to people everywhere! Today, in David's town, a Savior has been born. He is the Messiah you and your people have been waiting for; he is none other than the Lord. Here's how you will recognize him: go and seek out a newborn baby, swaddled and lying in a feeding trough. That will be the sign you've found him!"

Then it happened. Suddenly, a massive heavenly army appeared with the angel, and the entire legion began praising God, saying:

> In the heavens above, glory to God; and on the earth below, peace to those who please him!

When it was all over and the angels had returned to the heavenly realm, the shepherds looked at one another knowingly. "Forget the sheep!" one said. Another agreed: "Let's go to Bethlehem right now and see this amazing thing the Lord has revealed to us by his angelic servants!"

They ran into the village, and small as it was, it didn't take them long to find the new parents and their baby boy. It was just as the angel had told them. He was nestled down in a stone feeding trough.

Now that they had seen the Messiah, they went and told everyone they could find. Their joy was palpable, and everyone who heard their tale was astonished. Mary, the mother of Jesus, was peaceful and still through all of the excitement. She was storing it all up to make a memory she would cherish for the rest of her days. The shepherds returned to their field, praising the Lord and making much of him, for they knew he had given them a special honor: they had been the first to see the newborn Savior.

It was just as the prophet Isaiah said it would be:

> A child has been born to us! A Son has been given! Upon his strong back the governing of this world will rest.

> He will be known as the Counselor of Wonders and the God of Power, the Father to All Generations, and the Prince That Brings Us Peace.

> The splendor of his reign will know no end, and neither will the abundant life that spreads across his expansive domain.

> He will sit upon David's throne and rule the kingdom David was promised long ago; he will be its foundation and its security.

> Through his edicts he will dispense perfect justice, and right living will be the way of the world—from this moment in time on into eternity.

> The passion of the Lord of heaven will do all this! ✦

The Sign of the Manger

The feeding trough wasn't simply a makeshift cradle; it pointed to Jesus's purpose on earth.

"This will be the sign for you: You will find a baby wrapped tightly in cloth and lying in a manger." (Luke 2:12)

It's a peculiar scene, a baby asleep in a manger. It's really not very different from placing a modern newborn in the dog's food bowl for a nap. A manger was a feeding trough, a hollowed-out stone box where animals could find a bit of sustenance. In the lower room of the house where Mary gave birth, it became a makeshift cradle, but it was also a sign.

When an angel announced the birth of the Messiah to shepherds in a field outside of Bethlehem, the manger was part of the description. The angel told the terrified herdsmen the scene they would find in town: a baby wrapped in cloths and lying in a manger would be a sign for them. But what sort of sign?

The Bible is replete with signs that point beyond themselves to deep, spiritual realities. Often these signs are miracles. In Numbers 21, when God had Moses craft a bronze serpent and stick it up on a pole for every snakebitten Israelite to see, it was a sign pointing to Jesus, who would be pierced upon a Roman cross and become sin for us. Only by looking to the serpent were the people made well; likewise, only by looking to Jesus can any of us be forgiven and saved (John 3:14–15).

Sometimes, however, a sign is a prophetic act. Take, for example, the time God told the prophet Ezekiel to pack his bags in the sight of his fellow Jews, then dig a hole through a nearby wall before heading off into the night with his head downcast and his eyes covered (Ezek. 12:1–14). It was a bizarre scene, but it was symbolic of the coming exile. With Nebuchadnezzar's troops surrounding Jerusalem to starve the people, King Zedekiah and his army fled Jerusalem at night through a hole in the city's wall. But Zedekiah would be captured, his sons killed, and his eyes put out before being hauled away to Babylon (2 Kings 25:3–7).

In the case of baby Jesus in a manger, it was both a miraculous sign and a prophetic sign act. It was miraculous because the Son of God put on flesh and became one of us, being born of a virgin by the power of the Holy Spirit. The shepherds seeing the fully divine, fully human Christ child was the impossible made possible.

The Messiah in a manger was a living, breathing miracle, but his presence in the feeding trough was also a sign act. During his earthly ministry, Jesus said, "I am the living bread that came down from heaven. If anyone eats of this bread he will live forever. The bread that I will give for the life of the world is my flesh" (John 6:51). On the cross, Jesus laid down his flesh to bring salvation to the world. We "eat" his flesh and "drink" his blood by putting our trust in him, by taking his life into ours. Just as ingesting food nourishes the body and brings physical life, so feeding on Jesus nourishes the spirit and brings eternal life.

It's a difficult teaching, to be sure. The idea of devouring human flesh and blood is repulsive to us. But that's nothing new. It was a thought just as disgusting in Jesus's day. That is why, after Jesus said these things, "many of his disciples turned back and no longer accompanied him" (v. 66). And yet Jesus didn't soften his words for the crowd. He really is the only way of salvation. There is no life to be found without first partaking of his life.

It is not by accident that *Bethlehem* is Hebrew for "house of bread." In that small Judean village the Bread of Life was placed in a feeding trough as a sign to the world. In a few short decades, his flesh would be given as food for lost sheep. He would bring life to all those who hunger and thirst, not turning any away but welcoming everyone who comes to him to be satisfied: "And he took bread, gave thanks, broke it, gave it to them, and said, 'This is my body, which is given for you'" (Luke 22:19). ✦ ✦

The Sheep Left Behind

The sheep abandoned by the shepherds may be telling us more than we realized.

When the angels had left them and returned to heaven, the shepherds said to one another, "Let's go straight to Bethlehem and see what has happened, which the Lord has made known to us." (Luke 2:15)

In the ancient world, the job of a shepherd was simple. A shepherd led his flock to green pastures so the sheep could graze. He led them to streams so they could drink. He kept a watchful eye out for predators, and he brought back any strays that wandered off. His primary concern was keeping the sheep in his care safe. As such, the number-one rule of shepherding was fairly straightforward: don't abandon the sheep. And yet, that's precisely what the shepherds did on the night Jesus was born.

Of course, we can forgive these shepherds. They were visited by angels and told that the Messiah had been born. When the veil between heaven and earth is pierced by the glory of God, it has a way of rearranging one's priorities. As a group, the men headed into town to seek out the baby they had been told about. But behind them, in the darkness, the sheep were left to fend for themselves.

Why do these sheep matter? The truth is, they don't. And they didn't seem to matter much to the shepherds that night either. Luke tells us the men returned to their abandoned field, "glorifying and praising God for all the things they had seen and heard" (Luke 2:20). Their hearts were bursting with all the Lord had revealed to them; it's hard to imagine they gave more than a passing thought to the welfare of their sheep.

Ordinarily, this wouldn't be worth thinking about. But these may not have been ordinary sheep. You see, certain fields between Jerusalem and Bethlehem were reserved for tending the lambs used for temple sacrifices.[4] These sheep had to remain healthy and well cared for. They needed to be the best of the best because God required sacrificial animals without defect (Lev. 1:10; 3:1). And so, if these shepherds were tending the temple flock, it was no small thing to leave the sheep unattended.

Maybe they didn't realize what they were doing in the moment, but when those shepherds dropped their staffs and made a beeline for the baby Jesus, they were taking a step into a new era. In their world, sacrifices were essential for the people of Israel to draw near to God. But the blood of animals did nothing to remove their sin; it only covered it over for a time. The sacrificial system could not offer anyone forgiveness, eternal life, or a new heart. Something more was needed. And that something more was the newborn Babe they went to find.

> *Every priest stands day after day ministering and offering the same sacrifices time after time, which can never take away sins. But this man, after offering one sacrifice for sins forever, sat down at the right hand of God. . . . For by one offering he has perfected forever those who are sanctified.* (Heb. 10:11–12, 14)

The shepherds couldn't have known all that God had planned. They couldn't have known that the infant in the feeding trough would one day die for their sins. But it wasn't what they knew that had them marching toward Bethlehem that night; it was who they trusted. God had given them a Savior, the King and Messiah they had been waiting for their whole lives. And so they left behind the ninety-nine sheep in search of the one sheep that mattered, "the Lamb of God, who takes away the sin of the world!" (John 1:29). ✦ ✦

READING

Eight

THE BABY JESUS
IN THE TEMPLE

(Luke 2:21–39)

A PARAPHRASED RETELLING
OF LUKE 2:21–39

ON THE EIGHTH DAY following the baby's birth, Joseph and Mary had him circumcised in accordance with the law of Moses and God's instructions to Abraham. At that time they gave him the name Jesus, the name spoken to them by heaven's messengers.

Then, on the fortieth day, Joseph and Mary brought Jesus to the temple to present him before the Lord, once again following the law, which says, "Every firstborn male belongs to the Lord and is to be set apart as holy unto him." On that same visit, they also offered a sacrifice to restore Mary to a state of ceremonial purity after giving birth. It was the offering prescribed for the poor, "a pair of doves or young pigeons."

71

A man named Simeon had arrived sometime earlier, for he had been prodded by the Holy Spirit to visit the temple that day. Now, if there's anything to know about Simeon, it's that he was a lover of God, a holy man upon whom the Lord had placed his Spirit. In fact, the Holy Spirit had revealed to Simeon that death would not come for him until he had seen the Messiah with his own eyes; he would be blessed to see the Comforter of Israel in the land of the living.

When Joseph and Mary came into the temple with the baby Jesus, Simeon was overwhelmed and scooped the child up into his arms. Then he began to prophesy, saying:

> Lord of heaven and earth, my journey through this world can now end in peace. These old eyes of mine have seen your salvation, just as you promised!

> He is here for all to see, this child who will be the light of God's revelation for all nations, just as he will be Israel's glory!

Joseph and Mary were amazed at these words. But Simeon wasn't quite through. He turned to Jesus's mother and said, "This child will upset the balance of

power in Israel; many will be lifted high, but others will come crashing down—all because of him. His life will be a signpost from heaven, but even so, he will be opposed. In that conflict, the hearts of both the wicked and the faithful will be laid bare. And before it's all over, your own soul will be impaled, as if by the blade of a double-edged sword."

Also in the temple courtyard that day was a prophetess named Anna, whose family was from the tribe of Asher. Though Asher was among the ten tribes of Israel scattered and lost across the Assyrian Empire some seven hundred years prior, Anna's presence in the promised land was a living testament to God's promises to restore and to heal his people. And just like those promises, Anna was very old, having been a widow for eighty-four years. Even so, she wasn't alone, not in the slightest; she kept company with the Lord. In fact, she loved God so much, she never left the temple—her nights and days were filled with worship, fasting, and prayer.

When Anna spotted Jesus, she knew him instantly, and she thanked the Lord for the privilege of seeing Israel's newborn King. From that moment and for the rest of her days on this earth, she proclaimed

the arrival of the Messiah to every kindred soul in Jerusalem, to all those who were eager to see God's plan of redemption unfold in their day.

After Joseph and Mary had completed everything required by the law of the Lord, they returned to Bethlehem,[5] where they settled down to raise Jesus. ✦

The Welcoming Committee God Chose for His Son

God sees in people what the world often misses.

Now, Master, you can dismiss your servant in peace, as you promised. For my eyes have seen your salvation. (Luke 2:29–30)

When Joseph and Mary came to the temple, they offered a sacrifice for Mary's purification, something God's law required after giving birth. They had little means, so they opted for the offering of the poor: "two turtledoves or two young pigeons" (Lev. 12:8). Most likely, the couple purchased their birds from the temple merchants who had set up tables in the court of the Gentiles. Years later, Jesus would overturn those tables and drive the livestock away. He would turn to the men selling doves and say, "Get these things out of here! Stop turning my Father's house into a marketplace!" (John 2:16).

God had declared that his temple would be "a house of prayer for all nations" (Isa. 56:7), and yet the court of the Gentiles—the area designated for people from every nation—had become overrun with salesmen and animals and currency traders. There wasn't actually anything wrong with selling animals for the temple sacrifices. Imagine trekking miles and miles to Jerusalem for a festival with a lamb or a goat in tow. The animal would slow you down, and you'd be constantly worried that your unblemished animal would somehow be injured on the trip. The problem wasn't the selling of animals; it was where the sellers had set up their shops: inside the temple itself.

By buying animals already examined by the temple authorities and deemed worthy of sacrifice, worshippers could avoid having their offering rejected. The priests knew precisely what each sacrifice required. They could identify a proper lamb when one was set before them. Except this one time, when the Lamb of God—the Messiah they had been waiting for—was presented to them.

In addition to offering the sacrifice for Mary's purification, Joseph and Mary came to the temple to present Jesus and offer a payment for his redemption. Centuries earlier, when the spotless lambs were killed during the first Passover, it was in place of Israel's firstborn sons. God then decreed the firstborn sons of every mother in Israel belonged to him (Exod. 13:1–16). But they could be redeemed for five shekels of silver (Num. 18:16), and the tribe of Levi would take their place. And so, there in the temple, being redeemed for a few days' wages, was the sacrificial Lamb who would save not only the firstborn sons but all who called on his name.

But the priests didn't recognize him.

To be fair, there was nothing special about Jesus's appearance. He looked like any other Jewish baby. And it wasn't as though God had commanded the priesthood to stay on alert for a baby who would turn out to be the Messiah. Joseph and Mary simply did what any other new parents in ancient Israel would have done, and the priests did their jobs accordingly. But that doesn't mean Jesus wasn't recognized that day at the temple.

God had chosen two special people to identify the baby Jesus as the Savior God's people had been waiting for, and God's choice tells us something about his heart. Everything we know about Simeon and Anna, besides the fact they were both very old, has to do with what they gave to God and what God gave to them. Their lives were bound up in their trust of him.

Luke tells us Simeon was "righteous and devout." He feared God and walked according to his ways. And in an age when the Holy Spirit had not yet been poured out on all the faithful, "the Holy Spirit was on him" (Luke 2:25). The Spirit revealed things to Simeon (v. 26) and led him in his daily life (v. 27). Similarly, Anna was a prophetess (v. 36); she, too, enjoyed a relationship with the Holy Spirit.

Both were committed to waiting on the Lord. God had promised Simeon he would see the Messiah in his lifetime, and that had him "looking forward to Israel's consolation" (v. 25). We don't know how long he waited, but it may have been years or even decades. Based on Simeon's prayer when he saw the newborn Jesus—"Now, Master, you can dismiss your servant in peace" (v. 29)—it seems he was waiting for a good, long while. Anna, we're told, stayed in the temple "night and day with fasting and prayers" (v. 37). She, too, was totally devoted to her Lord.

To anyone who passed by Simeon or Anna, they would have seemed of little consequence—just two old-timers in the temple courts. But God saw them for who they were—his friends—and they were beautiful in his sight. So, when the fullness of time had come and God gave the world His Son, he chose Simeon and Anna to be part of the welcoming committee. ✦ ✦

READING

Nine

FROM ABRAHAM
TO JESUS

(Matthew 1:1–17)

A PARAPHRASED RETELLING
OF MATTHEW 1:1–17

NOW, THIS IS THE FAMILY TREE of Jesus the Messiah, the heir of David and the seed of Abraham:

It all began with Abraham, whom God called and promised to bless. Abraham was the father of Isaac, the son of promise.

Isaac was the father of Jacob, who struggled with God and prevailed.

Jacob was the father of the twelve tribes, including Judah, from whom a line of kings would come.

Judah sinned against his daughter-in-law Tamar, and Perez was born to him.

Perez was the father of Hezron, Hezron the father of Ram, and Ram the father of Amminadab.

Amminadab was the father of Nahshon, who was the head of the tribe of Judah during the sojourn in the wilderness.

Nahshon was the father of Salmon, who married Rahab, the prostitute-of-Jericho-turned-daughter-of-Yahweh.

Salmon was the father of Boaz, who married Ruth; she looked after her mother-in-law, Naomi, and God looked after her.

Boaz was the father of Obed, Obed the father of Jesse, and Jesse the father of David, a man after God's own heart who became king over all Israel.

David sinned with Bathsheba and murdered her husband, Uriah, and later Solomon was born to him.

Wise Solomon, who built the temple in Jerusalem, was the father of Rehoboam. But because Solomon became a fool and

allowed his heart to be seduced by other gods, God took the nation from Rehoboam and tore it in two.

Rehoboam was the father of Abijah, Abijah the father of Asa, and Asa the father of Jehoshaphat.

Jehoshaphat was the father of Jehoram, Jehoram the father of Uzziah, and Uzziah the father of Jotham.

Jotham was the father of Ahaz, who sacrificed his son in the fire to the dark gods.

Ahaz was the father of Hezekiah, who prayed to the Lord in his sickness and received fifteen more years of life.

Hezekiah was the father of Manasseh, who shed innocent blood and brought the Lord's reproach upon Jerusalem.

Manasseh was the father of Amon, who walked in his father's evil ways and was killed by his own servants.

Amon was the father of Josiah, who found the book of the law and tried to lead the people back to Yahweh.

Josiah was the father of Jeconiah, upon whom the destruction of Jerusalem and the exile to Babylon came.

Jeconiah was the father of Shealtiel, and Shealtiel the father of Zerubbabel, who led many Jews home to the land God had given them.

Zerubbabel was the father of Abihud, Abihud the father of Eliakim, and Eliakim the father of Azor.

Azor was the father of Zadok, Zadok the father of Akim, and Akim the father of Elihud.

Elihud was the father of Eleazar, Eleazar the father of Matthan, and Matthan the father of Jacob.

Jacob was the father of Joseph, the husband of Mary, to whom was born Jesus the Messiah, the King of the Jews!

By this reckoning, there were fourteen generations from Abraham to David, another fourteen from David to the exile, and fourteen more from the exile to the arrival of the long-awaited Messiah. ♦

Why Jesus Has Two Family Trees

Matthew and Luke both contain genealogies, and in the details lies the answer to an ancient mystery.

"Look, the days are coming"—this is the LORD's declaration—"when I will raise up a Righteous Branch for David. He will reign wisely as king and administer justice and righteousness in the land." (Jer. 23:5)

Everyone knows David loved to worship. He wrote nearly half the psalms in the Bible. He danced before the ark of the covenant, not caring what anyone but the Lord thought of him (2 Sam. 6:14–16, 21–22). He even erected his own tabernacle in Jerusalem to house the ark so he could enter it and spend time with God (6:17; 7:18). It should come as no surprise, then, that he desired to build the Lord a proper temple.

David made plans and even gathered materials and supplies for the building project. However, the man of worship was also a man of war, and in the end God told him, "You are not to build a house for my name because you are a man of war and have shed blood" (1 Chron. 28:3). The temple was instead built by David's son Solomon, whose reign knew unprecedented peace.

Even though David couldn't build God a house, God still wanted to build David one. The prophet Nathan announced to the king:

> "The LORD declares to you: The LORD himself will make a house for you. When your time comes and you rest with your

ancestors, I will raise up after you your descendant, who will come from your body, and I will establish his kingdom." (2 Sam. 7:11–12)

Now, the immediate fulfillment of this promise came at Solomon's coronation, when David's own flesh and blood sat upon his throne, giving him a dynasty. But ultimately these prophetic words pointed to Jesus, for God also said, "I will establish the throne of his kingdom forever" (v. 13). Only the kingdom of God is everlasting; only the Messiah of Israel will reign without end. And so, from David's time on, God's people looked for the Messiah to come from the royal line.

King after king arrived upon the scene, but none were the promised one. In fact, most were downright wicked, refusing to walk in the footsteps of their ancestor David, who was said to be a man after God's own heart (1 Sam. 13:14; Acts 13:22). Still, faithful Jews kept looking, kept waiting, kept holding on.

And then something happened: David's royal line was broken, shattered and cursed by God himself for all time. Jeconiah (Matt. 1:11), also known as Jehoiachin (2 Kings 24:6) and Coniah (Jer. 22:24), was one of the last kings of Judah, and he was a vile one. He only reigned for three months, but in that time he did great evil in God's sight—so much evil that God pronounced this sentence upon him: "Record this man as childless, a man who will not be successful in his lifetime. None of his descendants will succeed in sitting on the throne of David or ruling again in Judah" (v. 30).

This is why Isaiah rightly prophesied David's family tree would become "the stump of Jesse" (Isa. 11:1), Jesse being David's father. Stumps are dead. They're done. Nothing's going to grow. So, when we read Matthew's account of Jesus's lineage and see "Jeconiah fathered Shealtiel" in the mix (Matt. 1:12), alarm bells should go off. No one descended from Jeconiah could sit upon David's throne. None of them could claim to be king—not even Jesus.

The Messiah had to be a flesh-and-blood descendant of David, be born into Solomon's royal line, and also not be in Solomon's branch of the family tree because of Jeconiah. It was an impossible set of requirements. Thankfully, "impossible" has never been a problem for God. Just as God miraculously parted the waters and carved a highway through the middle of the sea, he produced a Branch from the dead stump of Jesse. In so doing, he kept his promise to David to give him a royal line through his son Solomon that would indeed last forever (see 1 Chron. 22:9–10).

Here's how he did it: As you may know, Matthew traces Jesus's lineage through Joseph, his earthly father. In Jewish law, the father's heritage was what mattered most. However, Jesus also had a lineage through his mother, Mary. In Luke 3:23–37, we see her side of the family. Mary is also descended from David (v. 31) but is not descended from Solomon; her family comes down through one of David's other sons, Nathan. That means Mary's line does not contain the curse of Jeconiah.

What's more, there was a stipulation in the law of Moses that if a man had no sons, his inheritance could be passed on to a daughter (see Num. 27:1–11). However, because the tribal allotments of land had to remain secure, that daughter had to marry within her own tribe (see Num. 36:5–13). Mary had no brothers, and when she married Joseph, also from the tribe of Judah, Joseph became her father's heir; that is why he is listed as the "son of Heli" (Luke 3:23; compare to Matt. 1:16, where Joseph is said to be Jacob's son). This legal reality made Jesus the heir to both sides of the family legacy.

Through his adoptive father, Joseph, Jesus is the rightful heir to Solomon's throne, and yet he is not part of Jeconiah's cursed bloodline. And through Mary, he is David's flesh and blood. Jesus is indeed the "Righteous Branch" (Jer. 23:5) from "the stump of Jesse" (Isa. 11:1). His family tree is a reminder that God always keeps his promises, even when those promises appear impossible to keep. ♦ ♦

READING

Ten

THE VISIT OF
THE MAGI

(Matthew 2:1–11)

A PARAPHRASED RETELLING
OF MATTHEW 2:1–11

AFTER TWO YEARS had passed, magi from the East ventured to Jerusalem in search of a newborn king. "Where is the king of the Jews who has been born?" they asked. "We saw his star when it rose in the sky and have come to worship him." But of course these wise men took notice of a new star in the sky, for as priestly astrologers, they studied the heavens above to discern the meaning of significant events on earth.

When this news of a star and a newborn king reached King Herod, he was rattled—and not only him, but all of Jerusalem too. So Herod convened a meeting of the city's religious experts, the chief priests, and the teachers of the law. He asked them where, according to the Scriptures, the Messiah was to be born.

They told him, "In Bethlehem of Judea, for God spoke through the prophet Micah and said:

> Bethlehem, city of David, though you are small among the towns of Judah, your importance is beyond measure!

> From your midst, a Shepherd King will arise to lead my people Israel."

After this, Herod summoned the magi in secret and deceived them into thinking that he, too, wanted to pay homage to the newborn king. By doing this, he discovered precisely when the star had first appeared in the sky—two years earlier. Then he encouraged his visitors to travel the short distance to Bethlehem and seek out the child: "Go quickly now and find the boy so that you can return and tell me where he is. Then I, too, will go and bow down before him."

This seemed good to the wise men, so they loaded up their caravan and went on their way. The star went ahead of them, moving across the night sky until it led them to a certain house in Bethlehem. The magi had finally arrived, and they were overcome with joy.

When they entered the house, they saw the Child in the embrace of his mother, Mary. Immediately, they fell down and worshipped him. Then they gave the boy King the treasures they had brought with them from the East, a small fortune in gold, frankincense, and myrrh. ✦

What's So Wise about Following a Star?

A new star appearing in the night sky meant something profound to people in the ancient world.

"Where is he who has been born king of the Jews? For we saw his star at its rising and have come to worship him." (Matt. 2:2)

A generation before Jesus, a star—or rather, a comet—lit up the night sky. Bright as it was, the people took it as a sign. Word spread quickly that the comet was the soul of Julius Caesar,[6] who had died earlier that year. "He must have been a god all along," they said to one another. Two years later, the senate officially recognized Julius Caesar as a god.

This all worked out nicely for Augustus, the adopted son of Julius Caesar, for if his father was a god, then that made him the son of a god. As such, he was viewed as a savior from above, the one who brings peace to the whole world. In that, his birth was "good news" (or "gospel") for people everywhere.[7]

With this bit of historical context in view, can you sense the subversive nature of the gospel accounts in the New Testament? Jesus is everything Augustus and the emperors who followed him pretended to be. His arrival is the real good news, not imperial propaganda. While Augustus was still reigning from Rome, the true Son of God was born in a small town on the edge of the empire. He was the long-awaited Savior the Jewish people had been waiting for, the "Prince of Peace" promised by God (Isa. 9:6). As such, his birth was heralded by angels as "good news of great joy that will be for all the people" (Luke 2:10). And a star in the sky above marked his birth—at least for those who knew to look up.

Matthew tells us that wise men in the East took notice of this new sparkle in the heavens. They understood that it was a sign announcing a new king had been born, and so they traveled to find him. These magi have become such an integral part of the Christmas story that we can easily forget we really don't know much about them. For starters, we don't know where in the East they were from. We also don't know how they were able to connect the new star in the sky with the birth of a Jewish king. We don't even know what compelled these men to pack up their things and head off on a monthslong adventure to pay homage to the young ruler. But if we work our way through these unknowns, connecting the dots, a beautiful picture of God's perfect planning begins to emerge.

It's hard to imagine these wise men traveled to visit every new king in the region. But something drew them to Judea. Perhaps they understood this was no ordinary king who had been born. Perhaps they understood this was not just a king but the Jewish Messiah, who was to rule "to the ends of the earth" (Ps. 72:8). Perhaps they had read that "all kings bow in homage to him, all nations serve him" (v. 11). Perhaps they marveled to learn that he would usher in a new age, one where the natural order of things would come undone, so that "the wolf will dwell with the lamb" (Isa. 11:6). Perhaps these Gentiles had learned from the Hebrew Scriptures. They had discovered the promises of God for the Jewish people—but not only for the Jewish people. And they believed.

Many Bible scholars believe these magi were from Babylon. And while the New Testament does not confirm or deny this, it's a theory that makes a lot of sense. First of all, Babylon is to the east of the promised land. Second, the region had a large Jewish population at the time of Jesus's birth. These were the descendants of the Jewish exiles who never returned to their homeland. Finally, if these magi were steeped in the traditions of their order, they may have stumbled upon the writings of their predecessor Daniel. The prophecies of Daniel, of course, contain much about the coming Messiah, certainly enough to pique the interest of astrologer-priests concerned about world events.

It may be that in their research they discovered that the star itself was prophesied more than a thousand years earlier. When the Israelites were sojourners in the wilderness, a seer for hire named Balaam attempted to curse them. But no matter how he tried, he wasn't able to do it. Instead of spewing curses, Balaam poured out blessings upon God's people. In one of them, he said:

> I see him, but not now; I perceive him, but not near.
> A star will come from Jacob, and a scepter will arise from
> Israel. (Num. 24:17)

We don't know how long the wise men pondered the star, trying to discern what it might mean, but it seems they did their homework. If they were from Babylon, the journey to Judea would have taken approximately four months (see Ezra 7:9). They told Herod the star appeared two years prior to their arrival (Matt. 2:7, 16). That means they would have had about twenty months to unravel the mystery before setting out in search of the King of kings. And unravel it they did, for when they finally found the child Jesus, "falling to their knees, they worshiped him" (v. 11). The wise men stayed but a short time in Bethlehem, and when they returned home, they left more than gold, frankincense, and myrrh behind; they also left us an example to follow.

According to every standard this world values, Augustus Caesar was worthy of celebration. He had fame and fortune, power and prestige—all the things one would expect a king and a god to have. But Caesar was powerless to bring true peace to the world, and no amount of money could free humanity from the curse of sin and death. On the other hand, Jesus's appearance and humble circumstances did nothing to suggest royalty or divinity, and yet the Word of God and a sign from heaven confirmed that he was the one upon whom all history would turn, the Savior the world desperately needed.

The magi believed God, and then they put their faith into action. They left behind the comfortable and the familiar to seek out the only one worthy of their worship. Today, we are called to do no less, even if it might seem foolish to the watching world. ♦ ♦

READING

Eleven

THE NIGHTMARE AFTER CHRISTMAS

(Matthew 2:12–15)

A PARAPHRASED RETELLING
OF MATTHEW 2:12–15

SOMETIME LATER, when the special visit was over, the magi returned home by a different route— one that avoided Jerusalem—because they had been warned in a dream not to have anything to do with King Herod.

Joseph, too, had a dream. In it, an angel of God told him, "Get out of bed! Quickly! Take Mary and Jesus, and head down to Egypt. It's no longer safe for you here in Judea. Herod wants the child dead, and he won't rest until he finds him!" And so, under the cover of night, Joseph did exactly as the angel commanded. He gathered his family and a few essential belongings and set out for Egypt. At the end of their journey, they found refuge from a murderous king in the same land their ancestors had found refuge from famine nearly two thousand years earlier.

When Herod realized the magi had double-crossed him, he flew into a rage. He ordered the execution of every male child in Bethlehem and the surrounding area—all the boys age two and under. (This was based on the timetable given to him by the magi when he asked about the star's appearance in the sky.) By this act of pure evil, Herod unwittingly fulfilled the words of the prophet Jeremiah:

> From a tomb in Ramah, the sound of mourning can be heard.
>
> Rachel sobs for her lost children; she weeps uncontrollably. There is no comfort on earth that can ease her pain because they are gone! ✦

When Darkness Invaded Christmas

Then Herod, when he realized that he had been outwitted by the wise men, flew into a rage. He gave orders to massacre all the boys in and around Bethlehem who were two years old and under. (Matt. 2:16)

"It's the most wonderful time of the year"—or at least that's how the song goes. But for many people, the holiday season brings fresh pain and disappointment. Lost loved ones, broken relationships, and longings not yet realized all contribute to the letdown that sometimes accompanies Christmas for these folks. In a season amplified by good tidings and great joy, the pains of this world can seem somehow sharper.

Jesus's birth ushered in a new age, but it did not obliterate the current one. The brightness of the Savior shines in the darkness, and yet the darkness is still fighting and thrashing in a futile attempt to regain its dominance. Take, for example, the murderous rage of Herod the Great. By all estimates, the wise men arrived near the end of the wicked king's life. History tells us that in those final years, paranoid Herod had three of his own sons killed to protect his throne.[8] And so, it should come as no surprise that when he was told a new "king of the Jews" had been born (Matt. 2:2), he resolved to murder him as well. A man who will destroy his own flesh and blood has little trouble ordering the deaths of those he does not know.

When the magi did not return to Jerusalem to give Herod the location of the child King, Herod decided to widen his net. He ordered the slaughter of every male child in the region of Bethlehem age two and under. Joseph,

Mary, and Jesus weren't there when armed soldiers raided homes and violently ended innocent lives. Tipped off by an angel, they were already on their way to Egypt.

Still, difficult questions remain: Why did God allow such a vile thing to happen? Why were there no angel dreams for the other residents of the Bethlehem community? No warning was given, no path of escape provided. For these other families, there was only tragedy and sorrow. How could a good God allow such evil, especially in connection with the birth of his Son?

Like Job before us, those who dig into these mysteries will not find an answer that clears up their confusion. Certainly, God does not rejoice in the deaths of innocent children (Exod. 20:13; Prov. 6:16–19). Undoubtedly, God is powerful enough to foil the plots of wicked men (Job 5:12; Ps. 33:10), and he has promised not to let the guilty go unpunished (Prov. 16:5; Rom. 2:8). And yet, God did not crush this evil on the spot. He did not intervene, except to save Joseph, Mary, and Jesus. And he has not explained himself to us.

More than two thousand years removed from the massacre in Bethlehem, we have our own tragedies and our own questions. We still experience loss and heartache. We still watch as wicked people devise their plots and hurt the innocent. We still see the darkness rage against the light, bringing misery and grief to those caught in its wake. And most of the time, God does not provide us with answers to placate our deepest hurts. We're left to wait in the coldness of the mystery.

That's not to say the Bible does not give us any answers. From the very beginning, God could have put an end to evil and sin and death with a word from his mouth. He could've crumpled up creation like a drawing that didn't turn out quite right, and he could've started over again. But he didn't. God, in his mercy, chose to work *within* this broken world. Rather than doling out instant judgment, he stayed his hand. Why? Because every human being is guilty. Every last one of us would have been destroyed.

At Christmas Jesus came, not to judge humanity but to save all those who would turn and cling to him as Savior and Lord (John 12:47). When Jesus began his earthly ministry, he proclaimed "the year of the Lord's favor" (Luke 4:19), a time of Jubilee when debts are forgiven. Now is the time to repent. Now is the time to turn from our selfish ways and rest in the loving arms of our King. We live in the space in-between. God's kingdom has come and is, right this moment, expanding across the earth. But it has not yet come in its fullness. We are caught in the midst of Jesus's prayer, "Your kingdom come. Your will be done on earth as it is in heaven" (Matt. 6:10). Those of us who love Jesus are working to bring the culture of heaven to earth, even as the culture of hell holds sway over so many.

One day Jesus will return, and there will be a reckoning. The darkness will be extinguished once and for all. Sin that has not already been paid for at Calvary will collect its wages, and death will die a final death. In our pain, we ask, "How long, Lord?" Because we have not known anything but this broken world with its mix of goodness and tragedy, we cry out for relief. We look forward to the day when "death will be no more" and when "grief, crying, and pain will be no more, because the previous things have passed away" (Rev. 21:4), when all things will be made right, and we wonder what's taking Jesus so long.

However, "the Lord does not delay his promise, as some understand delay, but is patient with you, not wanting any to perish but all to come to repentance" (2 Pet. 3:9). Our God would rather turn his enemies into sons and daughters than see them destroyed. If you balk at that idea, remember that you, too, were once an enemy of God. But he sent his Son to make a way for every wicked one of us to come home. And so, as we read the Christmas story in Scripture, we can wince at Herod's carnage, praying for the day when such scenes are no more, and we can thank God that he has held the door open for sinners of every stripe. ✦ ✦

READING

Twelve

THE ROAD
TO GALILEE

(Matthew 2:16–23; Isaiah 9:1–2)

A PARAPHRASED RETELLING
OF MATTHEW 2:16–23 AND ISAIAH 9:1–2

WHEN HEROD THE GREAT DIED, an angel of
the Lord shared the news with Joseph in a dream. He
said, "It's time to go! Take Mary and Jesus, and make
your own exodus from Egypt. Those who sought
the child's life are now dead and gone." Once again,
Joseph obeyed his marching orders from heaven.
And so, what the prophet Hosea had once said about
Israel rang true again: "I called my Son out of the
land of Egypt."

Joseph took Mary and Jesus and traveled north into
the promised land. But because Herod's ruthless
son Archelaus had been granted his father's throne
in Judea, they did not want to return to Bethlehem.
Apparently, God agreed with their feelings on the
subject because, in a dream, he warned Joseph to

avoid Judea. So the young family went home to Nazareth in Galilee. That is how Jesus became known as a Nazarene, the promised "Branch" (or in Hebrew, the *Nezer*) from the stump of David's family tree. In this way, God fulfilled the promise he made through the prophet Isaiah, that he would honor Galilee of the Gentiles with its paths around the sea, the land beyond the Jordan:

> The people wandering in darkness have seen a powerful light.

> A ray of brilliance has crested over the horizon for all those who live in the shadowlands. ✦

Bethlehem Bound

Joseph and Mary did not see their trip to Bethlehem as a short-term visit; rather, it seems they planned to relocate there permanently to raise Jesus in David's hometown.

But when he heard that Archelaus was ruling over Judea in place of his father Herod, he was afraid to go there. And being warned in a dream, he withdrew to the region of Galilee. Then he went and settled in a town called Nazareth. (Matt. 2:22–23)

Long before Mary received an angelic call to motherhood, the prophet Micah wrote, "Bethlehem Ephrathah, you are small among the clans of Judah; one will come from you to be ruler over Israel for me. His origin is from antiquity, from ancient times" (Mic. 5:2).

Though he "will come" (a future event), he is "from ancient times" because he was there with God at the beginning of all things (John 1:1). Properly understood, this is a prophecy about the Messiah, and faithful Jews in the ancient world knew this. Like his ancestor King David, the Lord's promised Messiah was supposed to come from Bethlehem.

Joseph and Mary undoubtedly knew this prophecy, especially since both of them could count King David as an ancestor. And so, when they learned they were to be the earthly parents of the Messiah, they must have wondered about the geography of the whole situation. Nazareth is nowhere near Bethlehem; the two towns are separated by about ninety miles of dusty terrain.

Then one day, the couple received word that Caesar Augustus had called for a census to be taken throughout the Roman Empire. The head of each household was required to travel to their ancestral hometown to register and be counted. Since Joseph was from the house and lineage of David, he had to travel to Bethlehem, the birthplace and childhood home of the king. It's not difficult to imagine Joseph turning to Mary and saying, "Ah! So this is how the Lord's getting us to Bethlehem! This is how the Messiah will be from David's town!"

In popular retellings of the Christmas story, the couple's journey to Bethlehem is usually depicted as a short visit. There's a good reason for this: an isolated reading of Luke's Gospel would lead us to believe that once the forty days for Mary's purification were complete and the proper sacrifices were offered at the temple, Joseph, Mary, and a bouncing baby Jesus were on their way home to Nazareth (Luke 2:39). But when we bring Matthew into the conversation, we're left with a problem: his Gospel has the family in Bethlehem some two years longer.

Despite what nativity scenes may show, the wise men were not there on the night of Jesus's birth. They showed up in Bethlehem about two years later. We know this because the magi told King Herod the star that announced Jesus's birth appeared in the sky two years prior to their arrival (Matt. 2:2, 16). Hence, this is why Herod, when he decided to murder the child who had been born King, slaughtered every boy in or around Bethlehem who was two years old or younger.

Apparently, Joseph and Mary took Micah's prophecy seriously and relocated to Bethlehem for the duration. It seems they came for the census and had no plans to return to Nazareth in Galilee afterward. They were, instead, going to raise Jesus in the hometown of his ancestor David. They must have thought, *If God's Word says the Messiah comes from Bethlehem, then we need to be in Bethlehem.* In obedience, they uprooted themselves and made a new life in Judea. Even upon returning from Egypt, where they had fled to escape the wrath of King Herod, Joseph had Bethlehem in his sights—that was, until he found out someone just as wicked as Herod the Great was reigning in Jerusalem:

> But when he heard that Archelaus was ruling over Judea in place of his father Herod, he was afraid to go there. And being warned in a dream, he withdrew to the region of Galilee. Then he went and settled in a town called Nazareth. (Matt. 2:22–23)

It was only because the Lord intervened that the family finally returned home to Nazareth. Joseph and Mary had understood God's will from the Hebrew Scriptures, and they did not deviate from their course until the Lord himself told them the time had come to leave Bethlehem for good. Whether they moved or stayed put, their first priority was to honor the Lord with their lives. Is it any wonder, then, that out of all the choices before him, these are the two people God chose to be the earthly parents of his Son? ✦ ✦

ABOVE ALL

(Colossians 1:15–20)

A PARAPHRASED RETELLING
OF COLOSSIANS 1:15–20

THE SON IS THE PERFECT IMAGE of the invisible God and is therefore the heir of all creation. All things were created by him—all that exists in the heavenly realm and all that exists on the earth—both seen and unseen, including spiritual and earthly rulers, powers, and authorities. All things were created by him and for him. He was there before all these things were made, and he stands above them all. In fact, nothing would continue to exist if not for him.

He is the head of the church, which is his body. And he is the beginning of a new creation, raised to life as the firstborn from among the dead, so that in everything, for all eternity, he might be exalted above all others. Just as God's glory filled the tabernacle in days gone by, God delighted to have the fullness of his deity take up residence in the Son's human body. And then, the Son went to the cross as the spotless

Lamb of God; his blood was shed to make peace between God and humanity. This had to happen so that all things—all that exists in the heavenly realm and all that exists on the earth—could be brought back into alignment with his goodness. ✦

The Christmas Dragon

The book of Revelation tells us that Jesus's birth sparked a war in the heavenly realm.

Then another sign appeared in heaven:

> There was a great fiery red dragon having seven heads and
> ten horns, and on its heads were seven crowns. (Rev. 12:3)

Tucked into the back of the Bible is an often overlooked bit of the
Christmas story. Though it seems worlds removed from the shepherds
and the wise men, the book of Revelation offers us a window into the
heavenly realm to reveal how the birth of Jesus shook the cosmos.

In a book filled with beasts, bowls, and blights, it's not surprising that the
birth of Jesus is portrayed using symbols and stars. Rather than a teenage girl named Mary, we find "a woman clothed with the sun, with the
moon under her feet and a crown of twelve stars on her head" (Rev. 12:1).
If you recall from the book of Genesis, Joseph had a dream where the sun,
moon, and stars represented his family (Gen. 37:9–11), who, at the time,
constituted the entire nation of Israel. This woman of the heavens, then,
is Israel, and she brings forth a son "who is going to rule all nations with
an iron rod" (Rev. 12:5). This child is Jesus, the true King of this world.
(The mention of an iron rod is a callback to Psalm 2, which is a Messianic
psalm and a prophecy about Jesus's reign.)

After this, a short statement sums up Jesus's life, ministry, death, resurrection, and ascension: "Her child was caught up to God and to his throne"

(v. 5). Just like that—blink and you'll miss it—Jesus's mission on earth is over, and he is seated at the right hand of the Father. The purpose of this vision, given to the apostle John, was to reveal mysteries, and so Jesus's time on earth is all but skipped over; it is not God's focus here. Instead, John's attention is drawn to a big, red dragon.

This tremendous beast has "seven heads and ten horns, and on its heads were seven crowns" (v. 3). It is powerful and vicious, the stuff of night-mares. But unlike many of the signs John sees in his vision, this one is iden-tified for us plainly: he is "the ancient serpent, who is called the devil and Satan, the one who deceives the whole world" (v. 9). Because of all Jesus has done, a great war erupts in heaven. The devil has lost his place—his right to accuse God's people—but he won't go willingly, so angel armies remove him by force.

To fully understand what is happening here, we need to back up a bit—all the way back to the book of Genesis. When Adam sinned in the garden, he yielded his God-given authority to the serpent. That is why Jesus could rightly refer to the devil as "the ruler of this world" (John 12:31; 14:30; 16:11). God gave Adam the authority to rule, and so Adam should have accused the serpent after the foul thing questioned the goodness of God, but he failed to do so. So now Satan accuses us humans of not living up to our identity as image bearers and vice-regents of God. Through these twisted barbs, the evil one ultimately targets the Lord himself, accusing God of not doling out justice as he should.

Jesus's death answered every accusation of the devil, once and for all. On the cross, God's wrath was poured out on the sins of all those who come to Christ. Then, at the resurrection, Jesus was vindicated. He had obeyed God perfectly in the places Adam had failed, and so he wrested back the mantle of authority that the first man laid down all those years ago. The devil no longer has the right to accuse humanity before the throne of God. This is why, in the book of Revelation, a full-blown war breaks out between Michael (along with his angels) and the devil (along with his underlings).

Satan refuses to go quietly and is cast down to earth, full of wrath and malice. We're told he has "great fury, because he knows his time is short" (Rev. 12:12). The kingdom of God has come, and it will one day fill the whole earth (Dan. 2:35, 44; Hab. 2:14; Rev. 11:15). Until it does, the devil will sow as much chaos as he can. He will bring as much pain and persecution to God's people as he can muster. That is why the apostle John can look around and declare that "the whole world is under the sway of the evil one" (1 John 5:19), even as those who put their trust in Jesus are "rescued . . . from the domain of darkness and transferred . . . into the kingdom of the Son" (Col. 1:13).

Now is not the time to ignore Satan, pretending he doesn't exist, as the people who love this world tend to do. Rather, it is a season to be vigilant, to resist the devil and his schemes, and have nothing to do with darkness (James 4:7; Eph. 5:12). The Lord has given us authority to take the gospel to the ends of the earth (Matt. 28:18–20; Acts 1:8), and he has put the church on the offensive; believers have been tasked with storming the very gates of hell (Matt. 16:18). So we do not need to live in fear. While the war continues, the devil's defeat is assured; the decisive battle was won by Jesus on the cross.

On that first Christmas, everything began to change. It was the day the woman clothed with the brightness of the sun gave birth to the child of promise. That event set in motion the undoing of darkness. After all, if there were no manger, there would have been no cross and no empty tomb. Today, we live in the aftermath of the war waged in the heavenly realm. To be sure, Satan is still "prowling around like a roaring lion, looking for anyone he can devour" (1 Pet. 5:8), but his accusations have been silenced. "Therefore, there is now no condemnation for those in Christ Jesus" (Rom. 8:1). And that is certainly good news. ✦ ✦

ABOUT THE AUTHOR

 John Greco is a Bible geek who has spent the bulk of his career futzing with words in the Christian publishing and ministry worlds. He is the author of several books, including *The Easter Lamb* (for children; forthcoming) and *The Ascent: A Devotional Adventure through the Book of Psalms*. He and his wife, Laurin, live just south of Nashville, Tennessee, where they daily wrangle their three boys and dream of someday getting to be the ones who take all the naps. John's website is johngrecowrites.com.

NOTES

1. The word denoting a lodging space is translated as "inn" in the KJV, NKJV, ESV, BSB, BLB, NASB, ASB, CEV, DRB, ERV, GWT, GNT, MSB, NAB, NET, NRSV, WBT, WEB, and WNT.

2. The word denoting a lodging space is translated as "guest room" in the CSB, NIV, LSB, and NHEB. Similarly, it is rendered "guest quarters" in the ISV and "guest-chamber" in the LSV and YLT.

3. Joel B. Green, *The Gospel of Luke*, New International Commentary on the New Testament (Grand Rapids: William B. Eerdmans, 1997), 128–29.

4. Paul H. Wright, "The Birthplace of Jesus and the Journeys of His First Visitors," in *Lexham Geographic Commentary on the Gospels*, eds. Barry J. Beitzel and Kristopher A. Lyle, Lexham Geographic Commentary (Bellingham, WA: Lexham Press, 2016), 6.

5. While the text of Luke 2:39 appears to indicate Joseph, Mary, and Jesus returned to Nazareth immediately after completing everything required by the law, Matthew reveals the family was in Bethlehem for two more years. See "Bethlehem Bound" on page 111 for more on this topic.

6. E. R. Bevan, "Deification," in *Encyclopedia of Religion and Ethics*, ed. James Hastings, John A. Selbie, and Louis H. Gray (Edinburgh; New York: T. & T. Clark; Charles Scribner's Sons, 1908–1926), 529.

7. These sentiments about Augustus are not speculation but are from a Roman edict, preserved in an inscription found in the Greek city of Priene (in modern-day Turkey) known as the Priene Calendar Inscription, dated to 9 BC.

8. H. Bond, "Herodian Dynasty," in *Dictionary of Jesus and the Gospels*, 2nd ed., eds. Joel B. Green, Jeannine K. Brown, and Nicholas Perrin (Downers Grove, IL; Nottingham, England: IVP Academic; IVP, 2013), 380.

NOTES, REFLECTIONS, OR FAMILY MEMORIES

Enjoy more B&H
Christmas and Advent Devotionals

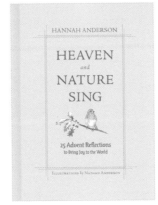

Devotionals for Upcoming Holidays

New Years

Easter

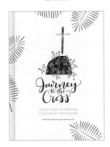

Mother's Day

Military Holidays

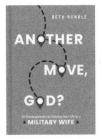

Devotionals for any time of year!

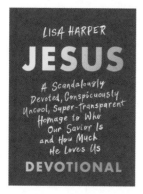

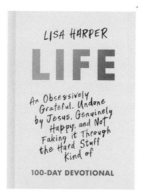

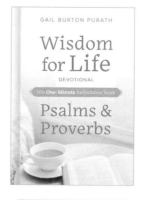

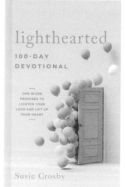